OVERCOMER

LIVE A LIFE OF UNSTOPPABLE
STRENGTH, UNMOVABLE FAITH,
AND UNBELIEVABLE POWER

DR. DAVID JE~~REMI~~AH

WITH DU~~?~~

W PUBLISHING GROUP

AN IMPRINT OF THOMAS NELSON

CONTENTS

INTRODUCTION

Let's face it: It's a difficult world out there. Sometimes it feels like our society is ripping apart at the seams. Sometimes it feels like our hearts can't take any more hurt. But no matter what the world throws at us—anxiety, fear, confusion, temptation—we have a choice on how to respond. We can concede defeat or live in the victory that God has promised to us in His Word.

Of course, it's easy to say we are going to choose victory. But it's another matter entirely to walk in it every day, especially when we are faced with problems that overwhelm us. I'm reminded of the story of David and Goliath as told in 1 Samuel 17. Day after day, the entire Israelite army was cowering in fear of the giant—including their king. It took a special kind of warrior to step into that situation and choose to be an Overcomer. David was that warrior. His trust in God was so secure that he *volunteered* to fight Goliath.

David had the conviction, courage, and confidence to face the giant. This was not due to the physical armor that King Saul tried to place on him—David actually refused to wear it—but because of the spiritual armor he had been equipping himself with every day as he spent time with the Lord. This enabled David to face his challenges in the strength of the Lord.

In this study, I want to teach you God's strategy for overcoming challenges so that you can be an Overcomer like David. To do this, we will draw on the apostle Paul's words in Ephesians 6:10–18 and discuss what it means to put on each piece of God's armor in a practical and effective way. As we go through each session, you will discover how to put on . . .

- the *belt of truth* to overcome falsehood
- the *breastplate of righteousness* to overcome evil
- the *shoes of the gospel of peace* to overcome anxiety
- the *shield of faith* to overcome fear
- the *helmet of salvation* to overcome confusion
- the *sword of the Spirit* to overcome temptation

Living the life of an Overcomer will bring you strength, peace, courage, hope, and joy such as you've never known. It will also bring victory in your spiritual life. So join me on this journey to *live a life of unstoppable strength, unmovable faith, and unbelievable power in the face of every challenge*. Embrace your God-given destiny—for you are an Overcomer!

HOW TO USE THIS GUIDE

The *Overcomer* video study is designed to be experienced in a group setting such as a Bible study, Sunday school class, or small group gathering. Each session begins with a brief "Welcome" section and opening questions to encourage thinking about the topic. After the opening questions, the group will watch the video message from Dr. David Jeremiah and engage in a time of directed discussion. Close each session with a time of personal reflection and prayer as a group.

During the week, maximize the impact of the study by engaging in the "Between-Sessions Personal Study" activities provided for that week. Treat each personal study section (*Seek, Reflect, Apply*) like a devotional, using the material in whatever way works best for your schedule. Note that these personal study sections are not required, but they will be beneficial to you in your progress toward becoming an Overcomer. Beginning in Session Two, there will be an opportunity to share any thoughts, questions, or takeaways you have from your personal study.

Each person in the group should have his or her own copy of this study guide. You are also encouraged to have a copy of the *Overcomer* book. Reading the book alongside the curriculum will provide additional insights and make the journey even more meaningful. To help you use both the book and this study, the "For Next Week" section lists the chapters in the *Overcomer* book that correspond to the following week's session.

Keep in mind that the video, discussion questions, and supplementary activities are simply tools to help you engage with each week's lesson. As you complete this study on becoming an Overcomer, be in prayer that you will discover all that God has for you—that you will no longer be defined by defeat, but will become an Overcomer who puts on "the whole armor of God," so that you can stand firm "against the wiles of the devil" (Ephesians 6:11).

Note: *If you are a group leader, there are additional resources provided in the back of this guide to help you lead your group members through the study.*

OVERCOMING FALSEHOOD WITH TRUTH

Truth is what fits us for the life of a Christian. Truth holds everything together and makes us ready. At the center of our lives we place "the truth [that] is in Jesus" (Ephesians 4:21). And everything we do is drawn from that all-encompassing center.

DR. DAVID JEREMIAH

WELCOME

You probably don't give much thought to the wardrobe staple known as the *belt*. For men, it's just something to keep their pants up and to match to their dress shoes if they want to look sharp. For women, it's more of a fashion accessory—an option among many to adorn an outfit. But in ancient times, a belt served a far more crucial role. Soldiers relied on their belts to hold all the other pieces of their armor together.

During the reign of the Roman Empire in the first century AD, most soldiers wore a shirt-like garment, a tunic, that covered their shoulders to their knees. Over this they placed metal armor and swaths of leather to protect their chest, arms, and legs. A band of thick leather bound their waist and provided loops to hold a sword, rope, rations, a money sack, and darts or other weapons. The belt provided a place for soldiers to store anything they might need—which was especially useful when engaging in hand-to-hand combat. The other items the soldiers needed to sustain their daily lives—canteen, food, coins—also remained within easy reach.

While the belt was not considered a piece of Roman armor, it ensured the rest of the soldiers' personal arsenal was organized and ready for action. A belt served as the foundation for their daily uniform, keeping everything in its place and providing a place for everything. When soldiers marched long distances or charged into a battle, they could "gird their loins," tucking their tunic into or around their belt to provide mobility for their legs.

Given this, it is little wonder that the apostle Paul's first instruction for us as Overcomers is to "stand therefore, having girded your waist with truth" (Ephesians 6:14). God's truth provides the foundation for the rest of our spiritual armor.

SHARE

If you or any of your group members are just getting to know one another, take a few minutes to introduce yourselves. Then discuss one of the following questions:

- What item serves the same function for you as a Roman soldier's belt? How does this item keep you organized for whatever you face each day?

— *or* —

- Why do you think God's truth is foundational to our lives as Overcomers in Christ? Why do you think Paul begins with this piece of spiritual equipment?

READ

Invite someone to read the passage below as everyone listens. Then pair up with someone sitting near you and answer the questions that follow. *Have done this as couples at Home*

> *Finally, my brethren, be strong in the Lord and in the power of His might. Put on the whole armor of God, that you may be able to stand against the wiles of the devil. For we do not wrestle against flesh and blood, but against principalities, against powers, against the rulers of the darkness of this age, against spiritual hosts of wickedness in the heavenly places. Therefore take up the whole armor of God, that you may be able to withstand in the evil day, and having done all, to stand. Stand therefore, having girded your waist with truth.*

EPHESIANS 6:10–14

11

1 According to this passage, why is putting on the full armor of God essential to your growth as a follower of Christ?

for protection against

✓ Truth holds every thing together

2 What comes to mind when you think of standing firm in today's culture? In your own daily life?

II Corinti 4 vs 2

WATCH ✳ *okay*

LISTEN

Play the video for Session One. As you watch, use the following outline to record any thoughts, questions, or key points that stand out to you.

Notes *Read*

We are under continual attack from an enemy who want to destroy our faith, our families, and our very lives. We need God's armor so we can face the reality of this opposition with *strength*.

Truth Holds Everything Together

Paul does not issue a call for us to *fight* but to *stand*. We are not told to fight because Christ has already defeated Satan. Putting on the armor of God equips us to be Overcomers.

David & Goliath fraical
3 spiritual atributes
overcomer

① refuse to be discouraged By your friends
② Reinforce your beleif in God

② Be sure to remember who you are representing
③ Reflect on your previous victories
④ Run Toward your problems

Paul begins with the belt of truth because Satan's major attack against believers is *falsehood* and *deception*.

against the truth in your Life

There are three ways people decide on what is "truth": *objective* truth, *relative* truth, and the *postmodern* position of truth.

No Longer exist
Jesus is & was Truth
Sprint
Truth as each people sees it
God is the Truth
For each of us creat for ourselfs
Truth is found iN GoD
① God of Truth

13

The first way we put on the belt of truth is by *seeking the truth* found in God's Word.

> We Need to study the Truth (Bible)
> Spirit of God Needs the Bible
> #1 - Bible Teaching study

The second way we put on the belt of truth is by *speaking the truth*.

> PROVERBS 6 ✓ God hates lying
> ① Tell the TRUTH - God called
> ② ✓ ✓ ✓ with LOVE & GRACE

> SPIN

③ The third way we put on the belt of truth is by *living the truth.*

> God wants us to Walk in Truth
> Seek & Live the Truth

Road

We need to equip ourselves with the belt of truth every day and in every situation. As we do this, we will become Overcomers in Christ.

me

DISCUSS

Read Eph 6-10-14

Take a few minutes with your group members to discuss what you just watched and explore these concepts in Scripture. Use the following questions to help guide your discussion.

1. What does it mean to you to "be strong in the Lord"? When have you experienced this in your life? How did it affect the way you were living your life?

   To Look to God for all situations

2. How would you describe the difference between *fighting* and *standing strong*? Why do you think believers are called not to fight but to take a stand against the enemy?

   Stand strong in the Truth & Don't Fight

3. How do the three umpires mentioned in the video teaching represent the three ways people today view "truth"? Provide an illustration where you have seen this view of truth displayed.

your interpertation

4. Why are our versions of truth not the same as God's divine truth? How are our views of truth limited in ways that God's truth is not?

God has the ultamate view or Truth

5. How has studying the Bible equipped you to stand in God's truth? When have you recently applied biblical truth to a situation you were facing?

See Romans 13

6. What does it mean to speak the truth in the context of your life right now? How can others see you living in God's truth?

RESPOND

Close out today's session by briefly reviewing the video teaching and any notes you took. Describe what it means to "gird your waist with God's truth." In the space below, write down the most significant point you took away from this session.

To always look for Gods Truth & live in it

PRAY

Conclude your time by sharing personal prayer requests, and then pray for these requests as a group. Ask God to work in each heart throughout the week and for the truths found in Session One, "Overcoming Falsehood with Truth," to become a reality in the life of each member.

PERSONAL STUDY

Take the material you have covered this week to a new level by engaging in some or all of the following between-session activities. Each of these activities will help you equip yourself with the belt of truth as you *seek* what God says in His Word, *reflect* on His truth, and *apply* what the Bible says to your life. Be sure to read the questions after each activity and write down your thoughts or key takeaways. There will be a time for you to share any thoughts you want to discuss with the group at the beginning of the next session.

SEEK

We live in an age of relativism, situational ethics, and lies—a world where people believe "truth" can be based on their own perspective or be whatever they create for themselves. Satan has been effective in his attacks against God's truth. Deception is a strategy he has employed since the Garden of Eden, as the following passage demonstrates:

Now the serpent was more cunning than any beast of the field which the LORD God had made. And he said to the woman, "Has God indeed said, 'You shall not eat of every tree of the garden'?"

And the woman said to the serpent, "We may eat the fruit of the trees of the garden; but of the fruit of the tree which is in the midst of the garden, God has said, 'You shall not eat it, nor shall you touch it, lest you die.'"

Then the serpent said to the woman, "You will not surely die. For God knows that in the day you eat of it your eyes will be opened, and you will be like God, knowing good and evil."

So when the woman saw that the tree was good for food, that it was pleasant to the eyes, and a tree desirable to make one wise, she took of its fruit and ate. She also gave to her husband with her, and he ate. Then the eyes of both of them were opened, and they knew that they were naked; and they sewed fig leaves together and made themselves coverings.

GENESIS 3:1–7

What was Satan's first strategy in causing Eve to doubt what God had said? Why did he initiate his attack with this question?

To question - did God realy say don't eat of the tree

What was Satan's second strategy in causing Eve to doubt God's truth? Why do you think his false claim was appealing to Eve?

You will not die: but be like God knowing good from evil.

What are some ways you see Satan using this same strategy today? Give an example from your life of when you have experienced the enemy twisting God's truth.

To go into battle with your enemy, you need to know the truth about God, the truth about Christ, and the truth found in the Bible. Read Hebrews 11:6. What is God's promise to those who diligently *study the truth* and *submit* to it? How are you doing this in your life today?

Those who seek God will find they are rewarded with his intimate presence.

REFLECT

Unfortunately, there's a sanctioned form of dishonesty in our world today called "spin." Spin is the recasting, reinterpretation, or revising of the truth to make it more palatable—and it's often used in politics. But in the Bible, we read of a government official who chose a different course:

> It pleased Darius to set over the kingdom one hundred and twenty satraps, to be over the whole kingdom; and over these, three governors, of whom Daniel was one, that the satraps might give account to them, so that the king would suffer no loss. Then this Daniel

distinguished himself above the governors and satraps, because an excellent spirit was in him; and the king gave thought to setting him over the whole realm. So the governors and satraps sought to find some charge against Daniel concerning the kingdom; but they could find no charge or fault, because he was faithful; nor was there any error or fault found in him. Then these men said, "We shall not find any charge against this Daniel unless we find it against him concerning the law of his God."

DANIEL 6:1–5

Daniel lived a life of honesty and integrity. How did this benefit him? What are some of the problems this caused for him?

Based on Daniel's story, what are some of the benefits and problems you might encounter as you follow God's truth?

If people looked at your life as the satraps did at Daniel's, what do you think they would say about you? Is there any area you feel you need to improve when it comes to integrity?

Read Proverbs 6:16–20 and Zechariah 8:16–17. Why is it so vitally important to speak the truth?

Because our Lord hates those that do not speak Truth

APPLY

Before we speak truth to others, Jesus made it clear we must begin with our own heart (see Matthew 7:5). Confession to God is a good way to open our heart to see His truth clearly and keep our focus on Him. The next step is to invite the Holy Spirit to examine and search our heart so we can be cleansed with the power of God's grace, like David did:

> *Search me, O God, and know my heart;*
> *Try me, and know my anxieties;*
> *And see if there is any wicked way in me,*
> *And lead me in the way everlasting.*

PSALM 139:23–24

Spend a few minutes asking God to search your heart and to reveal if there are any areas where the enemy has infiltrated your thoughts and life. Confess your sin and uncertainty to God and praise Him for the generous gift of His Son, Jesus Christ, who paid the penalty for your sin. If you need to go to someone else to ask for forgiveness, contact that person right away and begin the process. Remove all obstacles and footholds the enemy might try to use against you as you put on God's armor and grow in strength as an Overcomer.

FOR NEXT WEEK

If you are reading the *Overcomer* book as you complete this study, review chapters 1–3. In preparation for next week's study, read chapter 4, "Overcoming Evil with Good."

OVERCOMING EVIL WITH GOOD

It is by appropriating the righteousness of Jesus Christ—
His moral perfection and sinless life of obedience to the Father—
and living righteously that we are able to overcome the evil that is
within us and the evil that is around us.

DR. DAVID JEREMIAH

WELCOME

As we explored in the previous session, Paul first tells believers to "stand therefore, having girded your waist with truth" (Ephesians 6:14). Paul reminds us that we're not fighting *for* victory but *from* the victory Christ already secured for us at the cross. After establishing God's truth as our foundation, Paul then instructs us to "put on the breastplate of righteousness."

Compared to a belt, which we still use today, a breastplate might seem ancient and unfamiliar. But in Paul's day, it served a vital function for the Roman soldier: to protect his heart and vital organs—the core of his body. The modern equivalent of the breastplate is the ballistic vest, made of Kevlar or some other strong yet light-weight material, which law enforcement officials and military personnel wear when they are entering dangerous situations. When a bullet makes contact with the vest, the fibers absorb the impact and disperse the bullet's energy. Like the breastplate, this serves to protect the individual's heart and other vital organs.

The breastplate was an obvious and crucial form of protection in the first century AD. A warrior without a breastplate, or another form of protective armor, left his heart vulnerable and dangerously exposed to the enemy. In the same way, Paul states that a believer without a spiritual breastplate is leaving his heart open to the enemy's attacks. Only when we put on the righteousness obtained for us on the cross are we able to overcome evil with the goodness of God.

As we consider this challenge, we might be tempted to start by seeking victory over the evil that is so prevalent in the world around us. However, the Bible reminds us that we must first begin by overcoming the evil within our own hearts. Putting on the breastplate of righteousness equips us to confront evil on the *inside* as well as *outside* of us.

SHARE

Take a few minutes at the start of this session to go around the group and share any insights you have from last week's personal study. Then discuss one of the following questions:

- How do you keep your physical heart healthy? What practices, habits, or routines have you established to protect your heart from injury?

— *or* —

- What comes to mind when you think of the word *righteousness*? How would you define it to the group?

READ

Invite someone to read the passage below as everyone listens. Then pair up with someone sitting near you and answer the questions that follow.

> When He had called all the multitude to Himself, He said to them, "Hear Me, everyone, and understand: There is nothing that enters a man from outside which can defile him; but the things which come out of him, those are the things that defile a man. If anyone has ears to hear, let him hear!"
>
> When He had entered a house away from the crowd, His disciples asked Him concerning the parable. So He said to them, "Are you thus without understanding also? Do you not perceive that whatever enters a man from outside cannot defile him, because it does not enter his heart but his stomach, and is eliminated, thus purifying all foods?" And He said, "What comes out

of a man, that defiles a man. For from within, out of the heart of men, proceed evil thoughts, adulteries, fornications, murders, thefts, covetousness, wickedness, deceit, lewdness, an evil eye, blasphemy, pride, foolishness. All these evil things come from within and defile a man."

MARK 7:14–23

What surprises or stands out to you from Jesus' words in this passage? Why?

We are Not Defiled by what we eat. But by what we say & do

Stomack   Heart

It is the thought life that defiles you from your heart

How often do you think about evil being *within* you? What do you usually do when you see this within yourself?

fairly often
Talk to God

WATCH

Play the video for Session Two. As you watch, use the following outline to record any thoughts, questions, or key points that stand out to you.

Notes

When Paul uses the imagery of the breastplate of righteousness, he is reminding us that spiritually, it is righteousness that protects our hearts.

The Bible is clear that every man and woman has the seeds of evil growing within them. "There is none righteous, no, not one" (Romans 3:10).

We are Born with Sin

Christ, in His mercy, overcame the evil within us by dying on the cross and then offering us His righteousness—a gift we can only receive by faith.

GIVING

2 COR 5

Given your sin to christ

✓ How do we overcome Evil

Paul provides us with four strategies on how to overcome the evil around us. The first strategy is to *leave our vengeance with God.*

✓ Rom 12-17 to 21 *repay no one with evil*

Leave Vengence To God

overcome evil with Good

The second strategy is to *learn how overcoming works.*

✓ learn to plan ahead
Be Pro active

Rom 12 - vs 18

The third strategy is to *live peaceably with all people.*

Ask Jesus for help to the next Right Thing

- Let Good Overcome Evil

The fourth strategy is to *mitigate evil with good.*

✓ Let Good overcome Evil

Ask Jesus for Help

Love

Bless

✓ Love Your Enemy

When we repay evil with evil, we mirror what the culture and Satan would expect. But when we put on the breastplate of righteousness and repay evil with good, God is glorified by our actions.

✓ Love your Enemy

John Perkins'

DISCUSS

Take a few minutes to discuss what you just watched with your group members and explore these concepts in Scripture. Use the following questions to guide your discussion.

1. How do you respond to Paul's words, "There is none righteous, no, not one" (Romans 3:10)? What is the solution to the evil that is within our hearts? *Jesus is*

2. Why is it difficult *not* to extract vengeance from those who have hurt you? What is required in order for you to leave vengeance against your enemies to the Lord?

3. Is it easier for you to expect the best of other people or to assume you need to guard yourself against them? What has shaped this attitude within you?

4. What does it mean to *make plans* to do what is right in the sight of all people (see Romans 12:17)? In what way do you currently do this in your life?

5. What are some practical ways to live peaceably with all people? How can you be a person bearing God's peace to the people you interact with each day?

6. When have you personally witnessed someone repaying evil with good? What was the end result of that action?

RESPOND

Pause for a moment to reflect on the key points from this session. What does it look like for you to wear the breastplate of righteousness each day? Write down any takeaways or anything you want to pray about before the next session.

PRAY

Conclude your time together by sharing prayer requests. Before taking these requests to God in prayer, spend a few minutes praising and thanking God for the righteousness of Christ that covers our sin. Ask for His power and strength to love others—especially those who are difficult to love.

PERSONAL STUDY

Reflect on the material you have covered this week by engaging in some or all of the between-session activities below. Each of these activities will help you put on the breastplate of righteousness as you *seek* what God says in His Word, *reflect* on His truth, and *apply* what the Bible says to your life. Be sure to read the questions after each activity and write down your thoughts or key discussion points for the next group meeting.

SEEK

David, whom God chose to be His anointed king over Israel, was called a man "after His own heart" (1 Samuel 13:14). But David was also a sinner and often failed to equip himself with the breastplate of righteousness. His adultery with Bathsheba and subsequent cover-up is a reminder of our human capacity for yielding to temptation. Yet David experienced restoration through repentance. In Psalm 51, he penned these words to God:

Have mercy upon me, O God,
According to Your lovingkindness;
According to the multitude of Your tender mercies,
Blot out my transgressions.
Wash me thoroughly from my iniquity,
And cleanse me from my sin.

For I acknowledge my transgressions,
And my sin is always before me.
Against You, You only, have I sinned,
And done this evil in Your sight—
That You may be found just when You speak,
And blameless when You judge.

Behold, I was brought forth in iniquity,
And in sin my mother conceived me.
Behold, You desire truth in the inward parts,
And in the hidden part You will make me to know wisdom.

Purge me with hyssop, and I shall be clean;
Wash me, and I shall be whiter than snow.
Make me hear joy and gladness,
That the bones You have broken may rejoice.
Hide Your face from my sins,
And blot out all my iniquities.

Create in me a clean heart, O God,
And renew a steadfast spirit within me.

PSALM 51:1–10

How would you summarize David's requests to God?

Wants foregiveness

What is David's attitude toward himself in this passage?

GILT

What is David's attitude toward God? How does David believe God sees us?

As a sinner

Why does confession remain a vital part of your relationship with God even after you've accepted Jesus as your Savior and your sins have been forgiven?

REFLECT

The bad news is that we all have evil inside us. The good news is that Christ, in His goodness and mercy, overcame that evil by dying on the cross and offering us His righteousness. As John writes, "If we confess our sins, He is faithful and just to forgive us our sins and to cleanse us from all unrighteousness" (1 John 1:9). Spend a few moments today to consider where you are in your walk with the Lord. Then, using David's example in Psalm 51 as a model, write a prayer to God expressing your desire to know Him better and to remove any barriers between you. Don't worry about being eloquent or poetic—just write from the heart.

APPLY

Putting on the breastplate of righteousness not only allows you to receive the righteousness of Christ in faith but also to put His righteousness into practice by extending forgiveness to others. When you are equipped with this piece of spiritual armor, you have a heart that can overcome evil. Think about a person who has wronged you. You may not view him or her as evil or an enemy, but you are aware of how that person has wounded you. Read Romans 12:17–21, and then consider the following:

Have you forgiven that person? Why or why not?

Randy + Gary   yes

Are you seeking vengeance against that person in any way? If so, how will you put Paul's words in this passage into practice?

What are some ways you can respond to what they have done to you with the *goodness* of God?

Spend time in prayer, asking God to guide you and give you wisdom. Claim the protection of His whole armor through the righteousness of Christ. Then follow through on the action or conversation you believe God is encouraging you to have with that person.

FOR NEXT WEEK

If you are reading through the *Overcomer* book as you complete this study, read chapter 5, "Overcoming Anxiety with Peace," in preparation for next week's study.

OVERCOMING ANXIETY WITH PEACE

*If you struggle with anxiety, life can seem like a battle.
But God understands the extent of your worry. And because of
the gospel of peace, the one thing you don't have to fear is
losing His love. Even in the darkest nights of the soul, the God
of all peace is with you and for you.*

DR. DAVID JEREMIAH

WELCOME

Wingtips. Stilettos. Clogs. Sneakers. Sandals. Shoes are a multi-billion-dollar industry. Some consider them fashion essentials, while others collect them and have more than they will ever wear in a lifetime stored in their closet. Others only have a couple of pairs—one for work and one for dressing up. Most of us probably fall somewhere in between. But regardless of how many we own (or wish we owned), we all recognize the importance of wearing shoes.

So far in our exploration of the armor of God Paul described in Ephesians 6, we have discovered the importance of the belt of truth and the breastplate of righteousness. In this session, we turn to the next piece of spiritual equipment with Paul's instruction to "shod your feet with the preparation of the gospel of peace" (Ephesians 6:15).

The shoes Paul had in mind for his illustration probably resembled our modern-day football cleats more than penny loafers or sandals. Most soldiers in Paul's day wore open-toed leather boots with nail-studded soles for traction. These shoes were not made for running, hiking, or even necessarily for marching—even though they aided the Roman soldiers as they trudged across uneven roads and rocky terrain. The main function and purpose of the Roman shoe was rather to provide stability when the soldiers engaged in close fighting and hand-to-hand combat against an enemy.

The spiritual lesson Paul intends for us is clear: God's peace provides the stability we need in our lives as believers when we are standing against our enemy. The hectic pace of our society and the multitude of problems that come at us daily can leave us frantic with worry and exhausted from our efforts. This is where our enemy wants us to be: in a defeated state where we are constantly feeling anxious. But the Bible is clear that God wants us to have *His* peace.

SHARE

Take a few minutes at the start of this session to go around the group and share any insights you had from last week's personal study. Then discuss one of the following questions:

- How many different pairs of footwear do you own? What are some of the instances you would choose one pair over another?

— *or* —

- Why do you think Paul equates *peace* with *stability* in our lives?

READ

Invite someone to read the following passage as everyone listens. Then pair up with someone sitting near you and answer the questions that follow.

> *Therefore, having been justified by faith, we have peace with God through our Lord Jesus Christ, through whom also we have access by faith into this grace in which we stand, and rejoice in hope of the glory of God. And not only that, but we also glory in tribulations, knowing that tribulation produces perseverance; and perseverance, character; and character, hope. Now hope does not disappoint, because the love of God has been poured out in our hearts by the Holy Spirit who was given to us.*

ROMANS 5:1–5

How does God's peace provide a firm foundation for our lives even during trials?

What is one thing you're worried about right now? How can you put on the shoes of peace considering your concerns?

State of the World

WATCH

Play the video for Session Three. As you watch, use the following outline to record any thoughts, questions, or key points that stand out to you.

Notes

We have two kinds of peace available to us: peace *with* God and the peace *of* God.

We achieve peace *with* God when we come to faith in Christ and put our trust in Him.

John 14 - 27

We experience the peace *of* God as His calming presence carries us through the storms of life. This is the peace that "surpasses all understanding" (Philippians 4:7)—it is beyond our human logic.

God desires us to have both kinds of peace. Unfortunately, the gap between those who have made "peace with God" and those who have experienced the "peace of God" seems to be widening.

To equip ourselves with the shoes of the gospel of peace, we need to ask some important questions about our actions and habits. The first question is, *How are we praying?*

Phil 4 - 6+7

Matt 6 Lords prayer

Praise ① Progressive Prayer

Never skip the Worship • Pro-active Prayer

The second question we must ask is, *What are we thinking?*

Meditate on things

I am the gardian of our life

Isaih 26-vs 3

You can choose what you
Think about

The third question we must ask is, *Who are we following?*

Get a good friend

The fourth question we must ask is, *Where are we living?*

Past • Present   Future
Today

When will you find?
the peace

If we lace up the shoes of the gospel of peace each day, we will find that we can hold our ground against any assault that is thrown against us.

DISCUSS

Take a few minutes with your group members to discuss what you just watched and explore these concepts in Scripture. Use the following questions to help guide your discussion.

1. How would you explain the difference between peace *with* God and the peace *of* God to a new believer in Christ?

2. What are the greatest triggers you face each day that threaten your personal peace? How do you typically deal with those situations when they arise?

3. Remember a time in your life when you experienced the peace of Christ most keenly. How did His peace provide you with a secure, stable foundation from which to go forward?

4. How often do you pray to experience the peace of God? How would your life change if you prayed to feel God's peace each time you felt anxious or worried?

Phil. 4 vs 6to8

5. What are some ways you can share God's peace with others each day? What obstacles have you encountered when you have tried to share His peace?

6. How many of your worries today are related to past events and decisions? How many are related to future possibilities of what might happen? How can you stay grounded in the peace of Christ?

RESPOND

Pause for a moment to reflect on the key points covered during this session. What does it look like for you to wear the shoes of the gospel of peace? How can you experience the peace of God in your daily life? Write down any key thoughts or actions in the space below.

PRAY

If you are comfortable doing so, share one anxiety, worry, fear, or concern that is weighing you down. Then, as a group, take these requests to God in prayer. Conclude by thanking God for the gift of His peace and your ability to access it no matter what might be happening in your life.

PERSONAL STUDY

Reflect on the material you have covered this week by engaging in some or all of the following between-session activities. Each of these activities will help you to put on the shoes of the gospel of peace as you *seek* what God says in His Word, *reflect* on His truth, and *apply* what the Bible says to your life. Be sure to read the questions after each activity and write down your thoughts or key discussion points for the next group meeting. Use this personal study to provide fuel and nourishment to your soul as an Overcomer.

SEEK

With the constant pull of technology, the Internet, and social media, it can seem difficult these days to pause and experience God's peace. However, as we read the Psalms, we're reminded that events and calamities have always threatened to consume people's time and attention. Slowly read the passage on the next page, lingering over each word and phrase. Then reread the passage and answer the questions that follow.

LORD, my heart is not haughty,
Nor my eyes lofty.
Neither do I concern myself with great matters,
Nor with things too profound for me.

Surely I have calmed and quieted my soul,
Like a weaned child with his mother;
Like a weaned child is my soul within me.

PSALM 131:1–2

What do you think the psalmist means when he says that he is not concerned with great matters or "things too profound for me"?

How often do your own great and profound matters try to consume your thoughts and erode your peace?

How is experiencing the peace of God like a "weaned child with his mother"?

The child is dependant + relying on its mother
So we are with the Peace of God

In what way does this comparison illustrate how you can know God and enjoy His peace?

We must trust God
Realise what God has done for us

REFLECT

All too often, we allow discontent and dissatisfaction to rob us of peace. Paul reminds us, however, that this does not have to be the case. He writes:

> Not that I speak in regard to need, for I have learned in whatever state I am, to be content: I know how to be abased, and I know how to abound. Everywhere and in all things I have learned both to be full and to be hungry, both to abound and to suffer need. I can do all things through Christ who strengthens me.
>
> PHILIPPIANS 4:11–13

As Paul discovered, one way to overcome discontentment is by focusing on the many blessings that we have been given. When we realize just how much God has provided for us, we enjoy the peace that comes from a grateful heart. Today, take a few minutes in the space below to list ten specific things for which you are especially grateful for right now:

Share your list with at least one other person and tell him or her why you're grateful for what you have listed.

APPLY

Follow up with some of your group members this week and see how they are doing. Let them know you are praying for their request from the previous session. If your schedules permit, meet for coffee or lunch and share how you have been equipping yourself with the shoes of the gospel of peace this week. Also share what difference this has made concerning any fears, worries, or anxieties that you have been facing. Encourage one another to enjoy more of God's peace during the troubles and challenges that often come our way.

FOR NEXT WEEK

If you are reading the *Overcomer* book as you complete this study, read chapter 6, "Overcoming Fear with Faith," in preparation for next week's study.

OVERCOMING FEAR WITH FAITH

Faith is an active practice built on belief. Faith is not ambiguous; it's not unsure. It's a concrete conviction. It's the present-day confidence of a future reality. Faith is solid, unshakeable confidence in God built upon the assurance that He is faithful to His promises.

DR. DAVID JEREMIAH

WELCOME

Fear is a universal human experience. We all know the sensation we feel when life seems uncertain and out of control. Our heart races, our pulse quickens, and adrenaline courses through our body, causing us to react in a fight-or-flight mode. For such times, Paul calls on us to equip ourselves with the fourth piece of armor listed in our core passage: the shield of faith.

The Roman shield Paul had in mind protected infantry soldiers from their enemy during battle. These military shields were typically four feet tall and two and a half feet wide. They were made of leather stretched over wood and reinforced with metal at the top and bottom.

Of all the implements of warfare included in Paul's description of the Roman soldier, this is the only one given a specified purpose: "to quench all the fiery darts of the wicked one" (Ephesians 6:16). In ancient times, enemies would dip their darts in pitch, set them on fire, and shoot them into an enemy's camp in hopes of igniting it. Soldiers used their shields to protect their bodies from such fiery arrows and to stop the fire from spreading. In our case, the shield of faith protects us from "all the fiery darts of the wicked one."

Satan's goal has always been to get us to doubt the integrity of God. His intentions are not necessarily to hurt us physically but to cause us to question who God is and what He has said to us. Knowing his objective, we can see why *faith* is so important. If we stop believing who God is and what He has said, there is no way we can survive in the Christian life. We need the shield of faith to protect us from the enemy in his attempts to destroy our intimate relationship with our heavenly Father.

SHARE

Take a few minutes at the start of this session to go around the group and share any insights you had from last week's personal study. Then discuss one of the following questions:

- What is one thing that you're afraid of—spiders, snakes, heights, enclosed spaces, something else? What is your typical reaction when you encounter the things you fear?

— or —

- Why do you think Paul links *faith* to overcoming *fear*? How has your personal faith helped you to overcome your fears? *By remembering who God is and what he has done for me*

READ

Invite someone to read the passage below as everyone listens. Then pair up with someone sitting near you and answer the questions that follow.

Immediately Jesus made His disciples get into the boat and go before Him to the other side, while He sent the multitudes away. And when He had sent the multitudes away, He went up on the mountain by Himself to pray. Now when evening came, He was alone there. But the boat was now in the middle of the sea, tossed by the waves, for the wind was contrary.

Now in the fourth watch of the night Jesus went to them, walking on the sea. And when the disciples saw Him walking on the sea, they were troubled, saying, "It is a ghost!" And they cried out for fear.

But immediately Jesus spoke to them, saying, "Be of good cheer! It is I; do not be afraid."

And Peter answered Him and said, "Lord, if it is You, command me to come to You on the water."

So He said, "Come." And when Peter had come down out of the boat, he walked on the water to go to Jesus. But when he saw that the wind was boisterous, he was afraid; and beginning to sink he cried out, saying, "Lord, save me!"

And immediately Jesus stretched out His hand and caught him, and said to him, "O you of little faith, why did you doubt?" And when they got into the boat, the wind ceased.

Then those who were in the boat came and worshiped Him, saying, "Truly You are the Son of God."

MATTHEW 14:22–33

Imagine being with the disciples in the boat during the storm. Would you have been willing to walk on water like Peter? Or would your fear have kept you in the boat?

I would have been afraid

Why do you suppose Jesus sent His disciples ahead in the boat when He knew the storm was coming? Why would He deliberately put them in this situation?

To test their Faith

WATCH

Play the video for Session Four. As you watch, use the following outline to record any thoughts, questions, or key points that stand out to you.

Notes

Our faith in God is not based on superstition or mental assent. Rather, our faith reflects the invisible, eternal reality of our relationship with God through Christ.

Faith attitude based on facts

Faith is not *passive* but *active*. If we want to live as Overcomers, we must equip ourselves with the shield of faith and trust in the Lord.

There are four strategies that can help us grow in our faith. The first strategy is that *we need perspective.*

God has the Power

The second strategy to grow in our faith is to *hear the Word of God preached to us.*

Preaching

The third strategy to grow in our faith is to *understand that we need problems.*

Problems lead us to God

The fourth strategy to grow in our faith is to *be accountable to other people.*

Faith is like a muscle that grows when it is exercised, so God allows us to get into situations that require us to trust Him in unique ways that will stretch and strengthen our faith in Him.

Even when we come up against the enemy's darts of doubt and deception, we have no reason to fear. We can pick up our shield of faith and know the Lord is able to do above and beyond all that we could ever expect. He will protect us.

DISCUSS

Take a few minutes with your group members to discuss what you just watched and explore these concepts in Scripture. Use the following questions to help guide your discussion.

1. Do you believe that overcoming your fear is essential for your faith to grow? In other words, is it possible for your faith to increase *without* facing your fears? N1

   yes

2. When Peter "saw that the wind was boisterous, he was afraid; and [began] to sink" (Matthew 14:30). Was there a time in your life when you took your eyes off Christ and you started to sink? How did you change your focus?

3. What does it mean to have "faith as a mustard seed" (Luke 17:6)? Have you experienced a situation where you exercised a little faith and received big results?

4. Which of the four strategies for growing your faith do you regularly practice? How have they helped you face the fears in your life?

   We hear + read the Word

5. When have you been able to help another believer face their fears by reminding them of God's truth? When has someone else done the same for you?

   In preaching from the pulpit

6. Looking at your relationship with God, when has He allowed you to confront your fears in order to grow closer to Him?

RESPOND

As this session comes to a close, consider how you can encourage the others in your group to be Overcomers as you face your fears together and place your trust in the Lord. Write down anything you want to pray about or take action on before the next session.

PRAY

Conclude your time together by sharing any personal prayer requests, especially those involving your fears and the fiery darts the enemy is throwing against you right now. Take a few moments to pray silently, thanking God for His presence in your life. Then pray for one another in the group, remembering specific requests that have been shared. Be sure to praise God for His power and comforting protection from all that the enemy brings against you.

PERSONAL STUDY

Reflect on the material you have covered this week by engaging in some or all of the following between-session activities. Each of these activities will help you to put on the shield of faith as you *seek* what God says in His Word, *reflect* on His truth, and *apply* what the Bible says to your life. Be sure to read the questions after each activity and write down your thoughts or key discussion points for the next group meeting. Continue to reflect on what God is revealing to you as you pray and consider how to be an Overcomer.

SEEK

In the Bible, Hebrews 11 is often referred to as the "Hall of Faith." This is due to the way the author lists the faithful men and women of Scripture who trusted God, usually in impossible situations, and experienced His power and promises. These individuals overcame their fears and refused to succumb to the fiery darts of the enemy. Rather than doubt, they believed and stepped out in faith. Here are some of the individuals listed in this passage:

By faith Abel offered to God a more excellent sacrifice than Cain, through which he obtained witness that he was righteous, God testifying of his gifts; and through it he being dead still speaks.

By faith Enoch was taken away so that he did not see death, "and was not found, because God had taken him"; for before he was taken he had this testimony, that he pleased God. But without faith it is impossible to please Him, for he who comes to God must believe that He is, and that He is a rewarder of those who diligently seek Him.

By faith Noah, being divinely warned of things not yet seen, moved with godly fear, prepared an ark for the saving of his household, by which he condemned the world and became heir of the righteousness which is according to faith.

By faith Abraham obeyed when he was called to go out to the place which he would receive as an inheritance. And he went out, not knowing where he was going. By faith he dwelt in the land of promise as in a foreign country, dwelling in tents with Isaac and Jacob, the heirs with him of the same promise; for he waited for the city which has foundations, whose builder and maker is God.

By faith Sarah herself also received strength to conceive seed, and she bore a child when she was past the age, because she judged Him faithful who had promised. Therefore from one man, and him as good as dead, were born as many as the stars of the sky in multitude—innumerable as the sand which is by the seashore. . . .

By faith Isaac blessed Jacob and Esau concerning things to come.

By faith Jacob, when he was dying, blessed each of the sons of Joseph, and worshiped, leaning on the top of his staff.

By faith Joseph, when he was dying, made mention of the departure of the children of Israel, and gave instructions concerning his bones. . . .

By faith Moses, when he became of age, refused to be called the son of Pharaoh's daughter, choosing rather to suffer affliction

with the people of God than to enjoy the passing pleasures of sin,
esteeming the reproach of Christ greater riches than the treasures
in Egypt; for he looked to the reward. . . .

By faith the walls of Jericho fell down after they were encircled
for seven days. By faith the harlot Rahab did not perish with those
who did not believe, when she had received the spies with peace.

HEBREWS 11:4–12, 20–22, 24–26, 30–31

Which of these heroes of the faith stand out to you? What unique
characteristics about these individuals made an impact on you?

Noah

How do the examples of these people of faith speak to your fears?
What can you learn and apply from them to strengthen your shield
of faith?

If your name were listed here, what would you want the author
to say about you?

In what ways is your faith in God allowing you to lead a victorious life that might someday inspire others? Do you sense God is growing you in your faith? How?

REFLECT

Our fears tend to multiply when we dwell on them and allow them to have free rein. For this reason, instead of allowing our imaginations to run wild with speculation, what-ifs, and worst-case scenarios, we need to discipline our minds to focus on the power and goodness of God.

God's Word provides the remedy. As Paul writes, "[We cast] down arguments and every high thing that exalts itself against the knowledge of God, bringing every thought into captivity to the obedience of Christ" (2 Corinthians 10:5). A disciplined mind comes from trusting God in every situation and focusing on His eternal perspective instead of our own, which is limited by our finite comprehension.

On a separate piece of paper, make a list of whatever is consuming your attention against the knowledge of God. Then pray through each item on your list and take it before the Lord. Ask Him to help you relinquish its power over you. Then tear up your list and throw it away, thanking God that you can do all things through Christ who strengthens you.

APPLY

Write down several verses or passages on faith that especially encourage you. Some options include:

If you can believe, all things are possible to him who believes.

MARK 9:23

Have faith in God. For assuredly, I say to you, whoever says to this mountain, "Be removed and be cast into the sea," and does not doubt in his heart, but believes that those things he says will be done, he will have whatever he says.

MARK 11:22–23

So then faith comes by hearing, and hearing by the word of God.

ROMANS 10:17

For we walk by faith, not by sight.

2 CORINTHIANS 5:7

For by grace you have been saved through faith, and that not of yourselves; it is the gift of God, not of works, lest anyone should boast.

EPHESIANS 2:8–9

In this you greatly rejoice, though now for a little while, if need be, you have been grieved by various trials, that the genuineness of your faith, being much more precious than gold that perishes, though it is tested by fire, may be found to praise, honor, and glory at the revelation of Jesus Christ.

1 PETER 1:6–7

Place these verses where you will see them regularly during the week, such as on the corner of a mirror or window, in your car, on your desk at work, or on the kitchen counter or refrigerator. Use these verses to remind you of God's truth whenever you sense that a fiery dart of the enemy is being launched your way. Focus on the power you have been given in Christ to stand strong and be an Overcomer.

FOR NEXT WEEK

If you are reading the *Overcomer* book as you complete this study, read chapter 7, "Overcoming Confusion with Wisdom," in preparation for next week's study.

OVERCOMING CONFUSION WITH WISDOM

The wisdom of God equips and prepares you for God's purposes. It strengthens you in the certainty of your salvation so you can overcome confusion, falsehood, and uncertainty with the God-given confidence that comes through Christ alone. . . . There may be times when you're uncomfortable, in pain, and even sorrowful. But with the wisdom of God—which you gain by putting on the helmet of your salvation—you can overcome confusion.

DR. DAVID JEREMIAH

WELCOME

Whether it's a hardhat on a construction site, a motorcycle helmet, a hockey mask, or even a cap with a wide brim to guard against the sun's rays, headgear is an important item of self-protection. The same was true in Paul's day, where the right headgear for a soldier could mean the difference between life and death on the battlefield. It is little wonder then that our fifth piece of spiritual armor is the "helmet of salvation" (Ephesians 6:17).

Just as the breastplate protected a soldier's heart and vital organs, his helmet protected another vulnerable part of his body—his head. The typical Roman helmet was a leather cap reinforced with plates of metal. They often included a piece of metal in the back to protect the soldier's neck, a brow guard, and hinged cheek-protectors. Helmets for Roman centurions had a crest or plume on top, which enabled their fighters to find them in battle.

Regardless of the shape or construction of the helmet, the overall purpose was the same: to protect against fatal blows to the head. In the same way, God provides us with the helmet of salvation to protect our *minds* as we confront the enemy's attempts to confuse us. Satan recognizes that a negative thought or false idea has the potential to lead us down a spiral of destruction. For this reason, he often targets us with lies, deception, and confusion in the hopes of corrupting our beliefs or confusing our understanding of God's truth.

Today, we need the wisdom dispensed by God Himself. This wisdom allows us to know the course of action that will please God and make our lives what He wants them to be. While gaining this type of wisdom is not automatic, as we choose to put on the helmet of salvation each day, the Lord rewards our efforts to learn, grow, and improve.

SHARE

Take a few minutes at the start of this session to go around the group and share any insights you had from last week's personal study. Then discuss one of the following questions:

- When was the last time you wore a hat or some kind of headgear? What was the occasion? What was the purpose for wearing it?

— *or* —

- When was the last time you were confused by a situation or something someone said? How did you clarify your confusion?

READ

Invite someone to read the passage below as everyone listens. Then pair up with someone sitting near you and answer the questions that follow.

I beseech you therefore, brethren, by the mercies of God, that you present your bodies a living sacrifice, holy, acceptable to God, which is your reasonable service. And do not be conformed to this world, but be transformed by the renewing of your mind, that you may prove what is that good and acceptable and perfect will of God.

For I say, through the grace given to me, to everyone who is among you, not to think of himself more highly than he ought to think, but to think soberly, as God has dealt to each one a measure of faith.

ROMANS 12:1–3

What does it mean to be "transformed by the renewing of your mind"? Is this the same as putting on the helmet of salvation? Why or why not?

vs 2 *Let God change the way our minds think*

7 yes

How does a humble attitude—not thinking of yourself more highly than you ought—influence your thoughts and perceptions? How does humility protect your mind? *It Keeps our minds on God & not on our worldly self work*

WATCH

Play the video for Session Five. As you watch, use the following outline to record any thoughts, questions, or key points that stand out to you.

Notes

Our ability to acquire God's wisdom is not so much a matter of *doing* as it is of *being*. We have to prepare the ground of our mind so the seeds of God's wisdom can take root.

MIND OF CHRIST

There are six strategies on how to obtain God's wisdom and overcome confusion. The first strategy is to *have a devoted mind.*

God Provide protection #1 look for
Gods wisdom

wisdom vs Knowledge
is NOT
automatic about patience

Knowing to d the right thing
without president

The second strategy is to *have a dedicated mind.*

1 step — Know you need it (Humble Spirit)
2 step — Hungry soul
#3   Hungry heart us
     Hearing
#4   Heading mind do what he
                    tells us to do

Wise when we Keep Gods Word
     Must Seek the Wisdom

The third strategy is to *have a disciplined mind.*

Whole hearted

✓ We can loose our Spiritual Appitite

God will give you the wisdom
     if you Trust God   6.43 17
                               13
                               30

The fourth strategy is to *have a determined mind*.

The fifth strategy is to *have a diligent mind*.

The sixth and final strategy to overcome confusion is to *have a developing mind*.

We will strengthen our faith and protect our minds when we choose to put on the helmet of salvation and overcome confusion with God's wisdom and clarity.

DISCUSS

Take a few minutes with your group members to discuss what you just watched and explore these concepts in Scripture. Use the following questions to help guide your discussion.

1. How do your thoughts and intellect influence your faith? What role does your mind play in your relationship with God?

   If we get too proud of our self we loose our relationship with God

2. What kinds of thoughts tend to derail your faith? Memories of past mistakes? Self-criticism? Fear or anxiety over the unexpected? Judgment from others? Explain.

   Past mistakes

3. Which of the six strategies in the teaching stand out the most to you? Why? How can you practice this particular strategy in your daily life?

4. Why is studying and immersing yourself in God's Word important to your thinking? Why is it critical for protecting your mind?

5. How do your relationships influence your thinking? Who currently helps you by providing God's wisdom and clarity as you make decisions?

6. What has made the biggest difference in how you think about your faith since this study began? Why?

RESPOND

Pause for a moment to reflect on what stands out to you from this session. Consider what it means to put on the helmet of salvation in a practical way. What needs to change in your thinking in order to grow in your faith?

PRAY

Conclude your time together by going around the group and allowing each member to share his or her needs and requests. Then spend a few moments praying for one another. Ask the Lord to provide everyone with His wisdom and clarity of mind as you process and think through the material from this session.

PERSONAL STUDY

Reflect on the material you have covered this week by engaging in some or all of the following between-session activities. Each of these activities will help you to put on the helmet of salvation as you *seek* what God says in His Word, *reflect* on His truth, and *apply* what the Bible says to your life. Be sure to read the questions after each activity and write down your thoughts or key discussion points for the next group meeting. Ask the Holy Spirit to give you a clear mind and wisdom to dispel any negative thoughts or unhealthy patterns in your mind.

SEEK

During the teaching this week, you were given six strategies on how to acquire God's wisdom and overcome the confusion the enemy wants to put in your mind. Review each of these strategies on the following page and read the corresponding verse:

Have a devoted mind: *"You shall love the LORD your God will all your heart, with all your soul, and with all your mind"* (Matthew 22:37).

Have a dedicated mind: *"For 'who has known the mind of the LORD that He may instruct Him?' But we have the mind of Christ"* (1 Corinthians 2:16).

Have a disciplined mind: *"Therefore gird up the loins of your mind, be sober, and rest your hope fully upon the grace that is to be brought to you at the revelation of Jesus Christ"* (1 Peter 1:13).

Have a determined mind: *"Set your mind on things above, not on things on the earth"* (Colossians 3:2).

Have a diligent mind: *"Casting down arguments and every high thing that exalts itself against the knowledge of God, bringing every thought into captivity to the obedience of Christ"* (2 Corinthians 10:5).

Have a developing mind: *"And do not be conformed to this world, but be transformed by the renewing of your mind, that you may prove what is that good and acceptable and perfect will of God"* (Romans 12:2).

Which of these verses resonates with you the most? How is God speaking to your heart through this verse?

What needs to change in your thinking for you to better apply each of these strategies?

What does it mean for you to have the "mind of Christ"?

In order to develop the mind of Christ, do you need to focus more on devotion and diligence or on discipline and determination? Explain.

REFLECT

Read the following passage and consider the relationship between the thoughts you think and the words you speak to others.

> *Therefore, putting away lying, "Let each one of you speak truth with his neighbor," for we are members of one another. "Be angry, and do not sin": do not let the sun go down on your wrath, nor give place to the devil. Let him who stole steal no longer, but rather let him labor, working with his hands what is good, that he may have something to give him who has need. Let no corrupt word proceed out of your mouth, but what is good for necessary edification, that it may impart grace to the hearers. And do not grieve the Holy Spirit of God, by whom you were sealed for the day of redemption. Let all bitterness, wrath, anger, clamor, and evil speaking be put away from you, with all malice. And be kind to one another, tenderhearted, forgiving one another, even as God in Christ forgave you.*

EPHESIANS 4:25–32

In reviewing this passage, have there been any instances lately when you've let a "corrupt word" proceed from your mouth—words that did not "impart grace" to the recipient? Or is there someone in your life to whom you need to speak the truth in love? Prayerfully consider whom God is leading you to approach in this regard and what He would have you say to that person. Record your thoughts in the space below.

APPLY

The mistake many Christians make when seeking God's wisdom is to assume that, once found, it will enable them to see life from God's perspective. In truth, we're not shown God's long-term plans for us or how our actions today will impact those plans for tomorrow. But when we humble ourselves, God gives us the wisdom we need *for the moment.* Think about one item in your life that is causing you confusion and uncertainty today. Ask God to give you the wisdom you need *in this moment* to best handle that concern. Talk with other group members about the situation, and then follow through on the action you feel God is directing you to take.

FOR NEXT WEEK

If you are reading the *Overcomer* book as you complete this study, read chapter 8, "Overcoming Temptation with Scripture," and review chapter 9, "Overcoming Everything with Prayer," in preparation for next week's study.

OVERCOMING TEMPTATION WITH SCRIPTURE

Temptation affects everyone. It doesn't matter who you are, how strong you are, how knowledgeable, how immersed in the Bible, or how committed to integrity. To be Overcomers, we must constantly be on our guard because temptation is no respecter of persons.

DR. DAVID JEREMIAH

WELCOME

The stage has been set. The lines have been drawn. The enemy is real. Paul is clear that for believers, we will wrestle "against principalities, against powers, against the rulers of the darkness of this age, against spiritual hosts of wickedness" (Ephesians 6:12). However, as we have seen, God has given us the right equipment we need to stand strong.

As Overcomers, we are supported by the *belt of truth*. We are protected by the *breastplate of righteousness*. We have our feet shod with the preparation of the *gospel of peace*. We have been given the *shield of faith* and the *helmet of salvation*. We have the spiritual equipment we need to protect our hearts, our minds, and our souls from the enemy.

But as every soldier knows, it takes more than a good defense to win a fight. For this reason, the Lord has also given us an offensive weapon. As Paul writes, we are to take up "the sword of the Spirit, which is the word of God" (Ephesians 6:17). We have a mighty blade to cut through any obstacle that may try to block our spiritual progress!

The Roman soldier in Paul's day had a number of different weapons at his disposal, including javelins, spears, arrows, and even rocks fired in slings. But for close hand-to-hand combat, the preferred weapon was a short sword that closely resembled a dagger. The Greek word Paul uses for *sword* in this passage refers to that kind of dagger, which was anywhere from six to eighteen inches long.

Roman soldiers carried these long daggers in leather sheaths attached to their belts. With these at the ready, they were prepared at a moment's notice to not only defend themselves but to go on the offensive and overcome their foes. Similarly, for believers in Christ, the sword of the Spirit—which is the very Word of God—offers us a sharp and highly honed weapon that allows us to target our enemy's vulnerability.

SHARE

Take a few minutes at the start of this session to go around the group and share any insights you had from last week's personal study. Then discuss one of the following questions:

- What piece of armor listed by Paul in Ephesians 6:14–18 are you most in need of right now? Why that particular piece of equipment?

— *or* —

- Why do you think Paul compares the Word of God with a sword? Does that match the way you typically think of the Bible? Why or why not?

READ

Invite someone to read aloud the passage below as everyone listens. Then pair up with someone sitting near you and answer the questions that follow.

For the word of God is living and powerful, and sharper than any two-edged sword, piercing even to the division of soul and spirit, and of joints and marrow, and is a discerner of the thoughts and intents of the heart. And there is no creature hidden from His sight, but all things are naked and open to the eyes of Him to whom we must give account.

HEBREWS 4:12–13

How does the author describe the Word of God in this passage? What can it do?

How has the Bible illuminated God's truth in your life in the manner this author describes?

WATCH

Play the video for Session Six. As you watch, use the following outline to record any thoughts, questions, or key points that stand out to you.

Notes

There are two Greek words translated in English as *word*. *Logos* describes the complete revelation of God that we have in the Bible. *Rhema* refers to a specific saying of God—a passage that has application to a specific situation. → Saying of God

Jesus used the sword of the Spirit better than anyone. In Matthew 4:1–11, we see Him wield it with precision to overcome the devil's three temptations.

Jesus was Tempted
Devil Tempts us
1 God tests us to make us better

Satan's first temptation was to get Jesus to use His divine power to meet His human needs.

Duet 8 vs 3
1 Flesh   1 John 2 vs 16
2 eyes
3 pride of life

Satan's second temptation was to get Jesus to throw Himself from the top of the temple—and thus set Himself up as a wonder-worker.

Jump off the Temple
& God to save him
Do not tempt God
Satan will use the scripture

Satan's third temptation was to offer Jesus the kingdoms of the world if He would bow down before him. He was enticing Jesus to take a shortcut in reaching His goal. *Pride of life*

saying of God *Resist the Devil*

Jesus' example reveals three ways to wield the sword of the Spirit. The first strategy is to *stay in the line of fire*. *IMP*

The second strategy to wield the sword of the Spirit is to *be familiar with it.* *Search every part of Book*

Dueteronomy? *all scripture is God Given*

The third strategy to wield the sword of the Spirit is to *start collecting swords today*.

Memory is a gift of God
Born to be KINGS

Paul concludes his description of spiritual armor with an exhortation to be "praying always" (Ephesians 6:18). Prayer allows us to cry out to God in any situation and instantly have access to the resources of heaven.

DISCUSS

Take a few minutes with your group members to discuss what you just watched and explore these concepts in Scripture. Use the following questions to help guide your discussion.

1. Why do you think Paul saved the sword of the Spirit for last? How is it unique from the other pieces of armor that he has described?

2. Jesus could have rebuked Satan and instantly overcome any temptation. Given this, why do you think Christ chose to refute Satan's attacks by quoting Scripture?

Set an Example

3. When have you relied on God's Word to overcome a specific personal trial or temptation? What verse or passage helped you most in that situation?

4. What is one of your favorite verses or passages from God's Word when you're having a hard day? How are you building up your spiritual arsenal?

5. How does prayer complete your spiritual armor and enable you to become an Overcomer? Why is prayer just as essential as knowing God's Word?

6. How does prayer complement wielding the sword of the Spirit? How have prayer and Bible study uniquely equipped you for spiritual battle?

RESPOND

As you conclude your time together, turn to Ephesians 6:10–18 in your Bible and review Paul's words on the complete armor of God. Think about what you will take away from this study. What stands out the most to you from the material covered in these six sessions? Write down your thoughts and notes in the space below.

PRAY

Go around the group and allow each member to share what he or she has enjoyed the most from your time together. Share any requests or concerns that need to be lifted up as well. Close out the session and the study by taking a few minutes to praise the Lord as you celebrate putting on the whole armor of God and being Overcomers.

PERSONAL STUDY

Reflect on the material you've covered during this final week by engaging in any or all of the following activities. Each of these activities will help you to equip yourself with the sword of the Spirit as you *seek* what God says in His Word, *reflect* on His truth, and *apply* what the Bible says to your life. Think about all you've learned and how God has used your group experience to strengthen your faith and equip you for spiritual battle against the enemy.

SEEK

Throughout His time on earth, Jesus modeled for us what it looks like to be equipped with each piece of spiritual armor—truth, righteousness, peace, faith, and wisdom. But Jesus also knew how to wield the sword of the Spirit, which is the Word of God, when the enemy tried to speak his lies. In the following passage, we see how effective He was in responding to each of Satan's temptations with the truth of God's Word:

Then Jesus was led up by the Spirit into the wilderness to be tempted by the devil. And when He had fasted forty days and forty nights, afterward He was hungry. Now when the tempter came to Him, he said, "If You are the Son of God, command that these stones become bread."

But He answered and said, "It is written, 'Man shall not live by bread alone, but by every word that proceeds from the mouth of God.'"

Then the devil took Him up into the holy city, set Him on the pinnacle of the temple, and said to Him, "If You are the Son of God, throw Yourself down. For it is written: 'He shall give His angels charge over you,' and, 'In their hands they shall bear you up, lest you dash your foot against a stone.'"

Jesus said to him, "It is written again, 'You shall not tempt the LORD your God.'"

Again, the devil took Him up on an exceedingly high mountain, and showed Him all the kingdoms of the world and their glory. And he said to Him, "All these things I will give You if You will fall down and worship me."

Then Jesus said to him, "Away with you, Satan! For it is written, 'You shall worship the LORD your God, and Him only you shall serve.'"

Then the devil left Him, and behold, angels came and ministered to Him.

MATTHEW 4:1–11

On the following page, write down the three temptations that Satan brought against Jesus and the truth from God's Word that Christ used for His response.

<u>First temptation</u>   **<u>First truth</u>**

<u>Second temptation</u>   **<u>Second truth</u>**

<u>Third temptation</u>   **<u>Third truth</u>**

How can you draw on Christ's example and use the truth in God's Word as a way to resist whatever temptations you may be facing?

What specific verses or passages of Scripture can you cite against the enemy the next time he tempts you in these areas?

REFLECT

As we've seen, the Psalms provide poetic meditations on various aspects of our spiritual journey and relationship with God. Read through the passage from Psalm 119 and consider what God's Word means to you as you answer the questions that follow.

Oh, how I love Your law!
It is my meditation all the day.
You, through Your commandments, make me wiser than
    my enemies;
For they are ever with me.

I have more understanding than all my teachers,
For Your testimonies are my meditation.
I understand more than the ancients,
Because I keep Your precepts.
I have restrained my feet from every evil way,
That I may keep Your word.
I have not departed from Your judgments,
For You Yourself have taught me.
How sweet are Your words to my taste,
Sweeter than honey to my mouth!
Through Your precepts I get understanding;
Therefore I hate every false way.

Your word is a lamp to my feet
And a light to my path.

PSALM 119:97–105

What are some of the words and comparisons the psalmist uses to describe how he feels about God's Word? Which one best describes how you feel about the gift of God's Word?

What benefits have you experienced in your life by reading and studying the Bible? How can you continue to dig deeper into God's Word as nourishment for your spiritual growth?

Choose a favorite Bible verse and memorize it. Recite it to yourself, or others if you like, every day for one week. Then choose another verse and memorize it the following week. If you do this consistently, you will soon develop a habit of memorizing God's Word and be able to wield it effectively when temptations come your way.

APPLY

Consider what Bible study, group ministry, or service area God would have you participate in next. Keep in touch with others from this study group and see how you can encourage one another as you continue to grow in God's strength and power as Overcomers.

LEADER'S GUIDE

Thank you for your willingness to lead your group through this study! What you have chosen to do is valuable and will make a great difference in the lives of others. The rewards of being a leader are different from those of participating, and we hope that as you lead you will find your own walk with Jesus deepened by this experience.

Overcomer is a six-session study built around video content and small-group interaction. As the group leader, think of yourself as the host. Your job is to take care of your guests by managing the behind-the-scenes details so that when everyone arrives, they can enjoy their time together. As the leader, your role is not to answer all the questions or reteach the content—the video, book, and study guide will do that work. Your job is to guide the experience and cultivate your small group into a teaching community. This will make it a place for members to process, question, and reflect—not receive more instruction.

Before your first meeting, make sure everyone in the group gets a copy of the study guide. This will keep everyone on the same page and help the process to run more smoothly. If some group members are unable to purchase the guide, arrange it so that people can share the resource with other group members. Giving everyone access to all the material will position this study to be as rewarding an experience as possible. Everyone should feel free to write in his or her study guide and bring it to group every week.

SETTING UP THE GROUP

Your group will need to determine how long you want to meet each week so you can plan your time accordingly. Generally, most groups like to meet for either sixty minutes or ninety minutes, so you could use one of the following schedules:

SESSION	60 MINUTES	90 MINUTES
WELCOME (members arrive at the group and get settled)	5 minutes	5 minutes
SHARE (discuss one or both of the opening questions for the session)	5 minutes	10 minutes
READ (discuss the questions based on the Scripture reading for the session)	5 minutes	10 minutes
WATCH (watch the video teaching material together and take notes)	15 minutes	15 minutes
DISCUSS (discuss the Bible study questions based on the video teaching)	25 minutes	40 minutes
RESPOND / PRAY (reflect on the key insights, pray together, and dismiss)	5 minutes	10 minutes

As the group leader, you will want to create an environment that encourages sharing and learning. A church sanctuary or formal classroom may not be as ideal as a living room, because those locations can feel formal and less intimate. No matter what setting you choose, provide enough comfortable seating for everyone, and, if possible, arrange the seats in a semicircle so everyone can see the video easily. This will make the transition between the video and group conversation more efficient and natural.

Also, try to get to the meeting site early so you can greet participants as they arrive. Simple refreshments create a welcoming atmosphere and can be a wonderful addition to a group study. Try to take food and pet allergies into account to make your guests as comfortable as possible. You may also want to consider offering childcare to couples with children who want to attend. Finally, be sure your media technology is working properly. Managing these details up front will make the rest of your group experience flow smoothly and provide a welcoming space in which to engage the content of *Overcomer*.

STARTING THE GROUP TIME

Once everyone has arrived, it is time to begin the study. Here are some simple tips to make your group time healthy, enjoyable, and effective.

Begin the meeting with a short prayer and remind the group members to put their phones on silent. This is a way to make sure you can all be present with one another and with God. Next, give each person a few minutes to respond to the questions in the "Share" and "Read" sections. This won't require as much time in Session One, but beginning in Session Two, people will need more time to share their insights from their personal studies. Usually, you won't answer the discussion questions yourself, but you should go first with the "Share" and "Read" questions, answering briefly and with a reasonable amount of transparency.

At the end of Session One, invite the group members to complete the "Between-Sessions Personal Study" for that week. Explain that you will be providing some time before the video teaching next week for the group members to share their insights. Let them know sharing is optional, and it's not a problem if they can't get to these activities some weeks. It will still be beneficial for them to hear from the other participants and learn what they discovered.

LEADING THE DISCUSSION TIME

Now that the group is engaged, watch the video and respond with some directed small-group discussion. Encourage the group members to participate in the discussion, but make sure they know they don't have to do so. As the discussion progresses, follow up with comments such as, "Tell me more about that," or, "Why did you answer that way?" This will allow the group participants to deepen their reflections and invite a meaningful conversation in a non-threatening way.

Note that you have been given multiple questions to use in each session, and you do not have to use them all or even follow them in order. Feel free to pick and choose questions based on the needs of your group or how the conversation is flowing. Also, don't be afraid of silence. Offering a question and allowing up to thirty seconds of silence is okay. This space allows people to think about how they want to respond and gives them time to do so.

As group leader, you are the boundary keeper for your group. Do not let anyone (yourself included) dominate the group time. Keep an eye out for group members who might be tempted to "attack" folks they disagree with or try to "fix" those having struggles. These kinds of behaviors can derail a group's momentum, so they need to be steered in a different direction. Model active listening and encourage everyone in your group to do the same. This will make your group time a safe space and create a positive community.

The group discussion leads to a closing time of individual reflection and prayer. Encourage the participants to review what they have learned and write down their thoughts to the "Respond" section. Close by taking a few minutes to pray together as a group.

Thank you again for taking the time to lead your group. You are making a difference in the lives of others and having an impact on the kingdom of God.

ABOUT THE AUTHOR

David Jeremiah is the founder of Turning Point, an international ministry committed to providing Christians with sound Bible teaching through radio and television, the Internet, live events, and resource materials and books. He is the author of more than fifty books, including *A Life Beyond Amazing, Is This the End?, The Spiritual Warfare Answer Book, David Jeremiah Morning and Evening Devotions, Airship Genesis* Kids Study Bible, and *The Jeremiah Study Bible*.

Dr. Jeremiah serves as the senior pastor of Shadow Mountain Community Church in San Diego, California, where he resides with his wife, Donna. They have four grown children and twelve grandchildren.

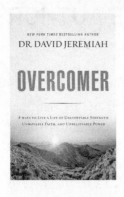

OVERCOMER

The idea of "overcoming" has transformed over time. When Christ came, the battlefield changed from plains and fields to the human mind and heart. In the *Overcomer* book, Dr. Jeremiah uses Paul's description of spiritual armor to teach us how we are called to overcome in this world of sin, explaining how, when we "put on" Christ, we can stand firm against the evil one.

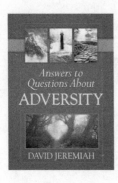

ANSWERS TO QUESTIONS ABOUT ADVERSITY

Throughout our lives, we often come up with many questions when we go through trials. During hard times, it's easy to wonder, "Why is life so hard?" The Bible has answers for us when we face adversity—but how are we to find them? *Answers to Questions About Adversity* is an instant source of eternal help, as it explains that, because Jesus defeated the Adversary, we can trust Him with adversities in our lives!

A.D. THE REVOLUTION THAT CHANGED THE WORLD

Have you every fully studied the events that surrounded the founding of the Early Church? Starting with the crucifixion of Christ, Dr. Jeremiah breaks down the events that took place and lead to the foundation of the global Church. Through this book, discover a magnificent portrait of the political and religious upheaval that occurred in those times and learn about one of the most significant times in world history.

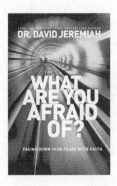

WHAT ARE YOU AFRAID OF?

Anxiety, fear, and worry are very common traits for many people today. There are many things to be afraid of, especially if your hope lies in the things of this world. But God has not called us to live in fear—but to live a life of joy and hope through Him! In *What Are You Afraid Of?* Dr. Jeremiah reminds us that, as Christians, we have been given all we need in order to face down even the most frightening obstacles in life. Through this book, learn to conquer the fears that are holding so many of us back from living the fullest for the Lord!